I fled Him,

down the nights

and down the days

I fled Him,
down the nights
and down the days

The text of "The Hound of Heaven"

by Francis Thompson

with photographic commentary

by ALGIMANTAS KEZYS, S.J.

and the text with interpretive commentary and annotations

by John F. Quinn, S.J., on pages 119-28,

the whole published by

LOYOLA UNIVERSITY PRESS

Chicago 60657

Printed in the United States of America

ISBN 0-8294-0195-4

Library of Congress Catalog Card Number: 72-137096

Design: William Nicoll, Edit, Inc.

I fled Him, down the nights and down the days;
I fled Him, down the arches of the years;

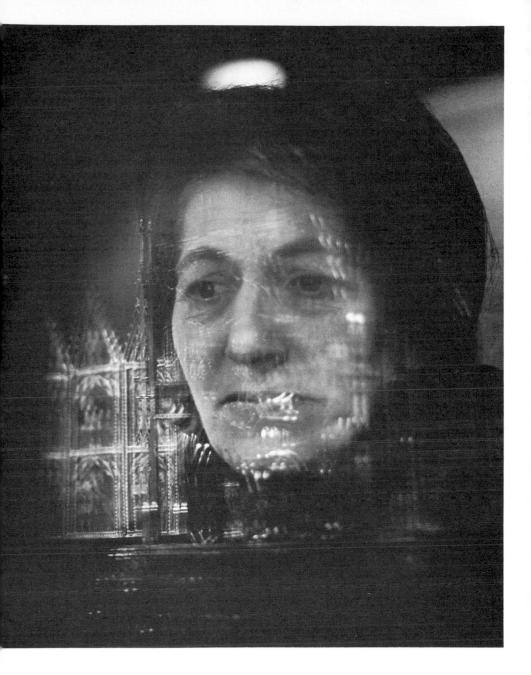

I fled Him, down the labyrinthine ways
    Of my own mind;

and in the mist of tears
I hid from Him, and under running laughter.

Up vistaed hopes I sped;

And shot, precipitated,
Adown Titanic glooms of chasmed fears,
From those strong Feet that followed, followed after.

But with unhurrying chase,
And unperturbèd pace,
Deliberate speed, majestic instancy,
They beat—and a Voice beat
More instant than the Feet—

"All things betray thee, who betrayest Me."

I pleaded, outlaw-wise,
By many a hearted casement, curtained red,
Trellised with intertwining charities;

(For, though I knew His love Who followèd,
    Yet was I sore adread
Lest, having Him, I must have naught beside.)

But, if one little casement parted wide,
  The gust of His approach would clash it to.
Fear wist not to evade, as love wist to pursue.

Across the margent of the world I fled,
　　And troubled the gold gateways of the stars,
　　Smiting for shelter on their clangèd bars;
　　　　Fretted to dulcet jars
And silvern chatter the pale ports o' the moon.

I said to Dawn: Be sudden—to Eve: Be soon;
  With thy young skiey blossoms heap me over
  From this tremendous Lover—

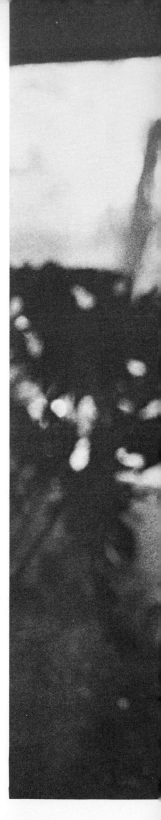

Float thy vague veil about me, lest He see!

I tempted all His servitors, but to find
My own betrayal in their constancy,
In faith to Him their fickleness to me,
   Their traitorous trueness, and their loyal deceit.

To all swift things for swiftness did I sue;
   Clung to the whistling mane of every wind.

But whether they swept, smoothly fleet,
The long savannahs of the blue;

Or whether, Thunder-driven,
They clanged his chariot 'thwart a heaven,
Plashy with flying lightnings round the spurn o' their feet:—
Fear wist not to evade as Love wist to pursue.

Still with unhurrying chase,
And unperturbèd pace,
Deliberate speed, majestic instancy,
Came on the following Feet,
And a Voice above their beat—

"Naught shelters thee, who wilt not shelter Me."

I sought no more that after which I strayed
In face of man or maid;

But still within the little children's eyes
    Seems something, something that replies,

They at least are for me, surely for me!
I turned me to them very wistfully;

But just as their young eyes grew sudden fair
With dawning answers there,

Their angel plucked them from me by the hair.

"Come then, ye other children, Nature's—share
With me" (said I) "your delicate fellowship;
    Let me greet you lip to lip,
    Let me twine with you caresses,

Wantoning
With our Lady-Mother's vagrant tresses,

Banqueting
With her in her wind-walled palace,
Underneath her azured daïs,

Quaffing, as your taintless way is,
From a chalice
Lucent-weeping out of the dayspring."

So it was done:

I in their delicate fellowship was one—
Drew the bolt of Nature's secrecies.

I knew all the swift importings
On the wilful face of skies;

I knew how the clouds arise
Spuméd of the wild sea-snortings;
   All that's born or dies
Rose and drooped with;

made them shapers
Of mine own moods, or wailful or divine;
With them joyed and was bereaven.

I was heavy with the even,
When she lit her glimmering tapers
Round the day's dead sanctities.

I laughed in the morning's eyes.

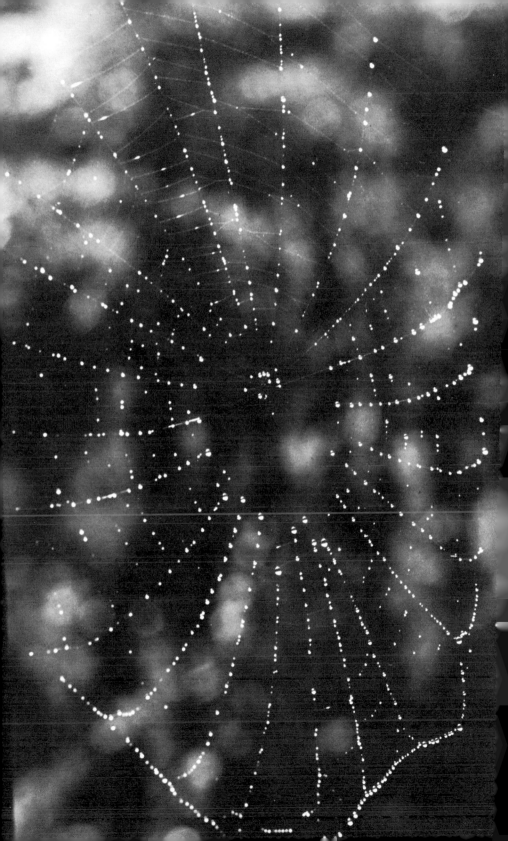

I triumphed and I saddened with all weather,

Heaven and I wept together,
And its sweet tears were salt with mortal mine;

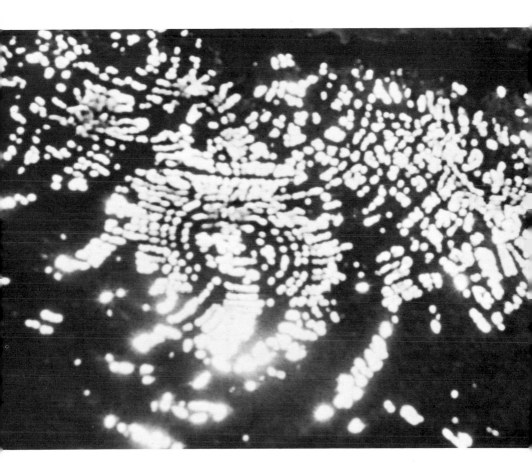

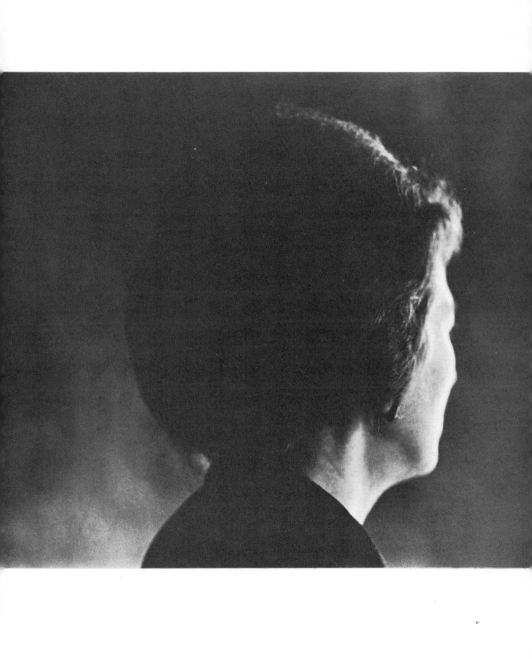

Against the red throb of its sunset-heart
      I laid my own to beat,
      And share commingling heat;
But not by that, by that, was eased my human smart.

In vain my tears were wet on Heaven's grey cheek.
For ah! we know not what each other says,

These things and I; in sound *I* speak—
Their sound is but their stir, they speak by silences.

Nature, poor stepdame, cannot slake my drought;
    Let her, if she would owe me,
Drop yon blue bosom-veil of sky, and show me
    The breasts o' her tenderness:

Never did any milk of hers once bless
    My thirsting mouth.

Nigh and nigh draws the chase,
With unperturbèd pace,
Deliberate speed, majestic instancy;

And past those noisèd Feet
A Voice comes yet more fleet—
"Lo! naught contents thee, who content'st not Me."

Naked I wait Thy love's uplifted stroke!
My harness piece by piece Thou hast hewn from me,
   And smitten me to my knee;
  I am defenceless utterly.
   I slept, methinks, and woke,
And, slowly gazing, find me stripped in sleep.

In the rash lustihead of my young powers,
      I shook the pillaring hours
And pulled my life upon me;

grimed with smears,
I stand amid the dust o' the mounded years—
My mangled youth lies dead beneath the heap.

My days have crackled and gone up in smoke,
Have puffed and burst as sun-starts on a stream.
　　　Yea, faileth now even dream
The dreamer, and the lute the lutanist;
Even the linked fantasies, in whose blossomy twist
I swung the earth a trinket at my wrist,
Are yielding; cords of all too weak account
For earth with heavy griefs so overplussed.

Ah! is Thy love indeed
A weed, albeit an amaranthine weed,
Suffering no flowers except its own to mount?

Ah! must—
Designer infinite!—
Ah! must Thou char the wood ere Thou canst limn with it?

My freshness spent its wavering shower i' the dust;
And now my heart is as a broken fount,

Wherein tear-drippings stagnate, split down ever
    From the dank thoughts that shiver
Upon the sighful branches of my mind.

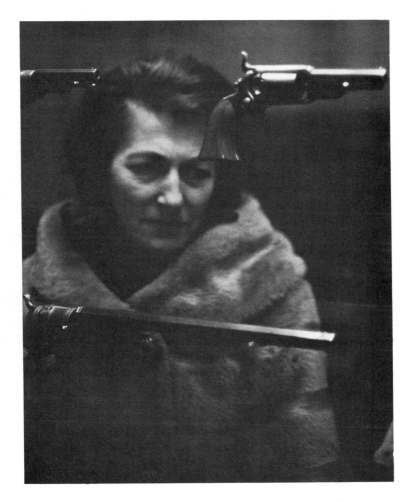

Such is; what is to be?
The pulp so bitter, how shall taste the rind?
I dimly guess what Time in mists confounds;

Yet ever and anon a trumpet sounds
From the hid battlements of Eternity;

Those shaken mists a space unsettle, then
Round the half-glimpsèd turrets slowly wash again.
    But not ere him who summoneth
    I first have seen, enwound
With glooming robes purpureal, cypress-crowned;
His name I know, and what his trumpet saith.

Whether man's heart or life it be which yields
Thee harvest, must Thy harvest fields
Be dunged with rotten death?

Now of that long pursuit
Comes on at hand the bruit;
That Voice is round me like a bursting sea:

"And is thy earth so marred,
Shattered in shard on shard?
Lo, all things fly thee, for thou fliest Me!

Strange, piteous, futile thing!
Wherefore should any set thee love apart?
Seeing none but I makes much of naught" (He said),
"And human love needs human meriting:

How hast thou merited—
Of all man's clotted clay the dingiest clot?

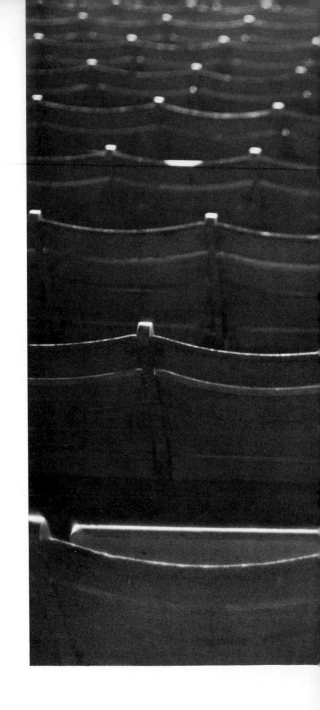

Alack, thou knowest not
How little worthy of any love thou art!

Whom wilt thou find to love ignoble thee
        Save Me, save only Me?

All which I took from thee I did but take,
  Not for thy harms,

But just that thou might'st seek it in my arms.

All which thy child's mistake
Fancies as lost,

I have stored for thee at home:

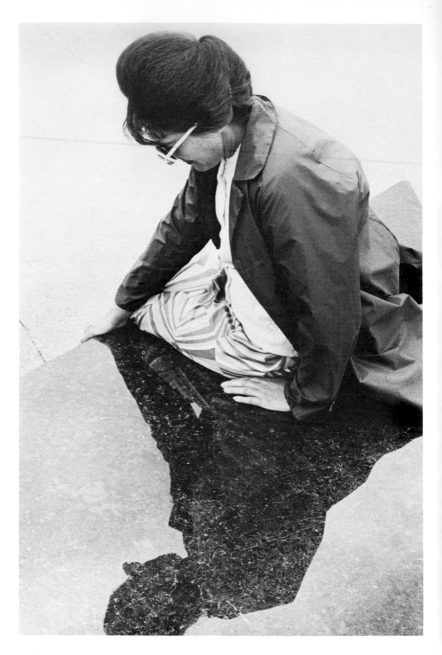

Rise, clasp my hand, and come!"

    Halts by me that footfall:
    Is my gloom, after all,
Shade of His hand, outstretched caressingly?

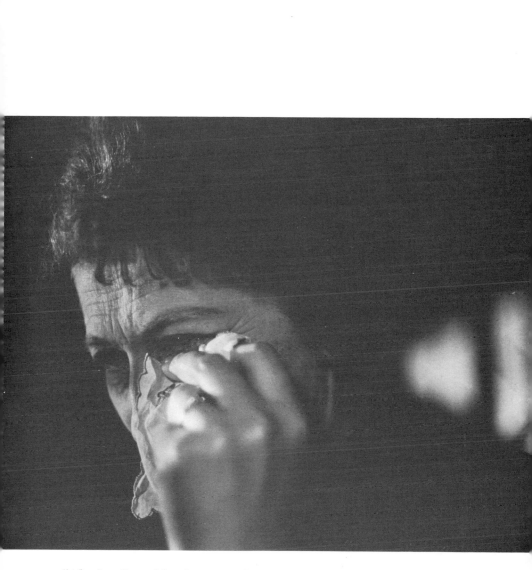

"Ah, fondest, blindest, weakest,

I am He Whom thou seekest!
Thou dravest love from thee, who dravest Me."

The Hound of Heaven

Francis Thompson

"The Hound of Heaven" is one of the great, if not the greatest, lyrical poems in the English language. For sublimity of thought, power of expression, beauty of imagery, and verse melody, all of which qualities are to be sought in a great poem, it is unsurpassed by any of the masterpieces of our greatest English lyrists.

Though the allegorical title may at first sight seem almost irreverent (God, the heavenly Hound, pursuing the fugitive hare, the soul), yet this metaphor really brings out with more telling force even than the comparison of the Good Shepherd and the lost sheep, the insistent, unrelenting search of God after the soul that is flying from his love and service. It expresses with great vividness the ceaseless energy, the insistence of the pursuit, and the almost mad desire for capture on the part of the pursuer, qualities so characteristic of divine love. This same thought it is that is brought out so powerfully by St. Ignatius in his *Spiritual Exercises.*

In this poem Thompson shows a mastery of the English language truly remarkable. Even the simplest thoughts he casts into figures of wondrous beauty, and one figure "doth tread upon another's heels, so fast they follow." The poem deserves the closest study. Besides the brilliance and originality of the imagery, note the complicated rhyming scheme, the rhetorical effects, tone color.

Though some critics think this poem may be a record of Thompson's own spiritual experience, this statement need not be taken literally. Poets as a rule are not accurate historians.

John Freeman in his essay on Francis Thompson in *The Moderns*, says: "*The Hound of Heaven* is one of the most wonderful lyrical poems in our language because it expresses an intense personality and a unique spiritual ardency. The poem is a striking instance of the co-existence of the two sincerities—the personal and the artistic; the joint activity of two motives—one spiritual and one poetic. . . . The pursuit of the soul by its 'tremendous Lover' has never been more purely or more powerfully suggested, even by the seventeenth-century poets with whom Thompson has so often been compared. Not Crashaw's self, vehement and storm-like as was his worship, has reached the sublimity of this tribute.

"And then, forgetting this, read the poem if you can simply as verse and note the height to which Thompson's muse so easily rises. He suggests, as few English poets do, speed, energy of flight, rapture. He uses repetition to sharpen the sense of pursuit: you hear the very wind of speed, feel the beating swift wings, are conscious of disturbed heights of air. Who since Shelley has moved more securely than Thompson among the large metaphors and images into which earthly and spiritual phenomena are resolvable and through which alone they are intelligible? Thompson rejoices in the spaciousness of imagery almost too great for comprehension. He is perhaps unique among poets of our generation who are masters of the sublime. . . . Only a poet of terrible earnestness and unchallengeable power dare attempt those fine-breathed flights in which anything short of perfect success is presumptuous failure. Thompson moves in the loftier altitudes with an ease which is in itself really impressive and absolute, the mark of royal inheritance. . . . This poem, for all the apparent exclusiveness of its subject, has really the universality of a great human conception, in which all men may see something, and many see more than the whole, of their private experience."

Note the many concrete figures to visualize the paths taken by the fugitive—arches of the years, labyrinthine ways, mist of tears, under running laughter, vistaed hopes.

I

I fled Him, down the nights and down the days;
   I fled Him, down the arches of the years;
I fled Him, down the labyrinthine ways
   Of my own mind; and in the mist of tears
I hid from Him, and under running laughter.
      Up vistaed hopes I sped;
      And shot, precipitated,
   Adown Titanic glooms of chasmed fears,
From those strong Feet that followed, followed after.
     But with unhurrying chase,
     And unperturbèd pace,
Deliberate speed, majestic instancy,
     They beat—and a Voice beat
     More instant[1] than the Feet—
"All things betray thee, who betrayest Me."

Day and night, through the years, in sorrow, joy, hope, and depression, the sinner fled from God, knowing all the while that he was being pursued. His conscience kept telling him that creatures would not satisfy his desire for love and happiness since he was betraying the Creator of them by flouting his love.

II

   I pleaded, outlaw-wise,[2]
By many a hearted casement, curtained red,
   Trellised with intertwining charities;
(For, though I knew His love Who followèd,
      Yet was I sore adread
Lest, having Him, I must have naught beside.)
But, if one little casement parted wide,
   The gust of His approach would clash it to.
Fear wist[3] not to evade, as love wist to pursue.

Like an outlaw begging for mercy, he pleaded for love from his fellowmen, but their love failed him while God still pursued.

1 *Instant*: Urgent.
2 *I pleaded* . . .: Here the sinner, pleading for the love of his fellowman, is compared to an outlaw pleading at a latticed window, the human heart being the window which is curtained in red, the symbol of love.

3 *Wist*: Knew, past of wit, to know, learn. The sinner in his fear knew not how to escape, as God in his love knew how to pursue.

Across the margent[4] of the world I fled,
　　And troubled the gold gateways[5] of the stars,
　　Smiting for shelter on their clangèd bars;
　　　　Fretted to dulcet jars
And silvern chatter[6] the pale ports[7] o' the moon.
I said to Dawn: Be sudden—to Eve: Be soon;[8]

Perhaps by getting out of the world entirely he might be able to escape the insistent pursuer, so in imagination he fled to the heavens, knocked at the gate of the stars, begging there for shelter. He bids the stars cover him and hide him from the pursuing lover. It is futile. There is no shelter for him there, for they are God's obedient creatures and will not betray him. The fugitive now realizes the truth of that saying in Psalm 138:
"If I go up to the heavens, you are there; if I sink to the nether world, you are present there."

With thy young skiey blossoms[9] heap me over
　　From this tremendous Lover—
Float thy vague veil about me, lest He see!
　　I tempted all His servitors, but to find
My own betrayal[10] in their constancy,

4　*Margent*: Limit, boundary.
5　*Troubled the gold gateways* . . . : His imaginative flight to the heavens is visualized and made concrete by comparing it to a man knocking at a gate, smiting on the bars for admission.
6　*Chatter*: A rattling.
7　*Ports*: Here, a gate; the same figure is applied to the moon. Note, however, the accurate contrast of description in the same figure applied to the golden stars and silver moon.

8　*I said to Dawn: Be sudden—to Eve: Be soon*: The natural and futile desire of a fugitive criminal, the speedy passing of time.
9　*Skiey blossoms*: The stars.
10　*My own betrayal*: Note the striking contrast expressed in these lines.

In faith to Him their fickleness to me,
   Their traitorous trueness, and their loyal deceit.[11]
To all swift things for swiftness did I sue;
   Clung to the whistling mane of every wind.[12]
      But whether they swept, smoothly fleet,[13]
   The long savannahs of the blue;
         Or whether, Thunder-driven,[14]
   They clanged his chariot 'thwart a heaven,
Plashy[15] with flying lightnings round the spurn o' their feet:—
   Fear wist not to evade as Love wist to pursue.
            Still with unhurrying chase,
            And unperturbèd pace,
      Deliberate speed, majestic instancy,
         Came on the following Feet,
         And a Voice above their beat—
   "Naught shelters thee, who wilt not shelter Me."

Swiftness alone will enable him to escape, so he clings to the swift wind and begs it to hurry him away. Again failure. Whether he be carried by the gentle zephyrs or the storm winds, the awful pursuer is at his heels, and he hears his warning words: "Nothing will shelter you because you will not shelter me."

III

I sought no more that after which I strayed
      In face of man or maid;
But still within the little children's eyes
   Seems something, something that replies,
They at least are for me, surely for me!
I turned me to them very wistfully;
But just as their young eyes grew sudden fair
      With dawning answers there,
Their angel plucked them from me by the hair.[16]

Dissatisfied with his fellowmen he turns to the fascinating, innocent love of children. Here he will find repose. But just as the little children begin to respond to his love, Death takes them from him Again disappointment.

11 *Traitorous trueness, loyal deceit*: A form of antithesis in which contradictory terms are brought sharply together for the sake of emphasis. It is called oxymoron.
12 *Clung to the whistling mane of every wind*: His escape on the swift winds is strikingly visualized by likening it to the escape of a man on a fast horse.
13 *Whether they swept, smoothly fleet*: The gentle zephyrs.
14 *Thunder-driven*: The storm winds, visualized as a team of racing steeds, their chariot driven by Thunder.
15 *Plashy*: Note the awful sublimity of this line, so typical of Thompson who, even more perhaps than Shelley, loved to romp in vast spaces.
16 *Their angel plucked them from me by the hair*: Death.

IV

"Come then, ye other children, Nature's—share
With me" (said I) "your delicate fellowship;
Let me greet you lip to lip,
Let me twine with you caresses,
Wantoning
With our Lady-Mother's vagrant tresses,
Banqueting
With her in her wind-walled[17] palace,
Underneath her azured daïs,[18]
Quaffing, as your taintless way is,
From a chalice
Lucent-weeping[19] out of the dayspring."[20]
So it was done:
I in their delicate fellowship was one—
Drew the bolt of Nature's secrecies.[21]
I knew all the swift importings
On the wilful face of skies;
I knew how the clouds arise
Spumèd of the wild sea-snortings;
All that's born or dies
Rose and drooped with; made them shapers
Of mine own moods,[22] or wailful or divine;
With them joyed and was bereaven.
I was heavy with the even,

In despair he turns to the children of Nature and begs admittance into their intimate fellowship. They receive him, he becomes a child of Mother Nature, knows her secrets, shares her joys and sorrows. Here, he thinks, is love and happiness. But it is neither lasting nor real. He soon tires of Nature. She is powerless to fill the void and satisfy the longing in his heart. Again he hears the footfall of the pursuer, deliberate and insistent as ever, and he catches his words of warning and entreaty: "Nothing will content you because you will not content me."

17 *Wind-walled*: A beautiful expression for out-of-doors, the home of Mother Nature.
18 *Dais*: Canopy. *Azured dais*: The sky.
19 *Lucent-weeping chalice*: A chalice pouring out light.
20 *Dayspring*: The early dawn.

21 *Drew the bolt of Nature's secrecies*: Had an intimate knowledge of the workings of Nature, expressed in particular in the lines that follow.
22 *Made them shapers of mine own moods*: This expresses in general his sympathetic knowledge of Nature, particularized in the following lines.

When she lit her glimmering tapers
Round the day's dead sanctities.
I laughed in the morning's eyes.
I triumphed and I saddened with all weather,
        Heaven and I wept together,
And its sweet tears were salt with mortal mine;
Against the red throb of its sunset-heart[23]
        I laid my own to beat,
        And share commingling heat;
But not by that, by that, was eased my human smart.
In vain my tears were wet on Heaven's grey cheek.
For ah! we know not what each other says,
        These things and I; in sound *I* speak—
Their sound is but their stir, they speak by silences.
Nature, poor stepdame, cannot slake my drought;[24]
        Let her, if she would owe me,
Drop yon blue bosom-veil of sky, and show me
        The breasts o' her tenderness:
Never did any milk of hers once bless
            My thirsting mouth.
        Nigh and nigh draws the chase,
        With unperturbèd pace,
    Deliberate speed, majestic instancy;
        And past those noisèd Feet
        A Voice comes yet more fleet—
"Lo! naught contents thee, who content'st not Me."

---

23 *Against the red throb of its sunset-heart*:
From this line down to "My thirsting
mouth" the relation between the fugitive
and Mother Nature in whom he has taken
refuge is visualized by the relation be-
tween a mother and her infant child.

24 *Cannot slake my drought*: Cannot satisfy
my thirst for love and happiness.

V

Naked I wait Thy love's uplifted stroke!
My harness piece by piece Thou hast hewn from me,
       And smitten me to my knee;
    I am defenceless utterly.
    I slept, methinks, and woke,[25]
And, slowly gazing, find me stripped in sleep.
In the rash lustihead of my young powers,
    I shook the pillaring hours[26]
And pulled my life upon me; grimed with smears,
I stand amid the dust o' the mounded years—
My mangled youth lies dead beneath the heap.
My days have crackled and gone up in smoke,
Have puffed and burst as sun-starts[27] on a stream.
    Yea, faileth now even dream
The dreamer, and the lute[28] the lutanist;
Even the linked fantasies,[29] in whose blossomy twist
I swung the earth a trinket at my wrist,
Are yielding; cords of all too weak account[30]
For earth with heavy griefs so overplussed.
    Ah! is Thy love indeed
A weed, albeit an amaranthine weed,[31]
Suffering no flowers except its own to mount?

There is nothing left now but surrender. Like a defeated gladiator, stripped of his armor, he kneels before the divine Conqueror, a captive. In a dream he sees his past life wasted in foolish flight and vain pursuits. Everything has failed him; nothing has satisfied his desire for love and happiness. Even the poetry in which he used to find so much consolation cannot now content him. It is trifling and transitory. He must have a love great and lasting. God will not permit him to love creatures and exclude divine love from his heart.

---

25 *I slept, methinks, and woke*: He is given a retrospect of his wasted life.

26 *I shook the pillaring hours*: A reference to Samson, the strong man, of the Old Testament (Judges 1:30), who by shaking the pillars of the house in which the Philistines were banqueting, pulled down the building, destroying all within it, including himself. "In the rash lustihead of my young powers, I shook the pillaring hours," that is, in the vigor of his youth, instead of serving God, he squandered his time in vain pursuits, thus shaking and pulling down the whole temple of time to his own destruction.

27 *Sun-starts*: An unusual word; the sun-lit bubbles that appear on the water.

28 *Lute*: The lute of poesy on which the poet plays.

29 *Fantasies*: Poetic fancies, figures in which the poet used the earth, stars, and the planets as his playthings. Here they are visualized as a chain pendant from his wrist on which he dangles the earth.

30 *Cords of all too weak account*: The consolation afforded him by poetry cannot equal the sorrows of this life.

31 *Amaranthine weed*: An imaginary never-fading flower that absorbs all the moisture near it, causing flowers nearby to die.

Ah! must—
        Designer infinite!—
Ah! must Thou char the wood[32] ere Thou canst limn with it?
My freshness spent its wavering shower i' the dust;
And now my heart is as a broken fount,
Wherein tear-drippings stagnate, split down ever
        From the dank thoughts that shiver
Upon the sighful branches of my mind.
        Such is; what is to be?
The pulp so bitter, how shall taste the rind?
I dimly guess what Time in mists confounds;
Yet ever and anon a trumpet sounds
From the hid battlements of Eternity;
Those shaken mists a space unsettle, then
Round the half-glimpsèd turrets slowly wash again.
        But not ere him who summoneth[33]
        I first have seen, enwound
With glooming robes purpureal, cypress-crowned;
His name I know, and what his trumpet saith.
Whether man's heart or life it be which yields
        Thee harvest, must Thy harvest fields
        Be dunged with rotten death?

God, the infinite artist, must perfect his creature, man, by trial and suffering before he is a fit instrument for divine use. The captive is repentant and grief-stricken at his misspent youth. He sees in the dim future death awaiting him.

32 *Char the wood*: As the artist must reduce the wood to charcoal before it is a fit instrument for drawing, so God must purify the soul by trial and suffering to make it a fit instrument for divine use.

33 *Him who summoneth*: Death.

VI

Now of that long pursuit
  Comes on at hand the bruit;[34]
That Voice is round me like a bursting sea:
  "And is thy earth so marred,
  Shattered in shard on shard?[35]
Lo, all things fly thee, for thou fliest Me!
Strange, piteous, futile thing!
Wherefore should any set thee love apart?
Seeing none but I makes much of naught" (He said),
"And human love needs human meriting:
  How hast thou merited—
Of all man's clotted clay the dingiest clot?
  Alack, thou knowest not
How little worthy of any love thou art!
Whom wilt thou find to love ignoble thee
  Save Me, save only Me?
All which I took from thee I did but take,
  Not for thy harms,
But just that thou might'st seek it in my arms.
  All which thy child's mistake
Fancies as lost, I have stored for thee at home:
  Rise, clasp my hand, and come!"

  Halts by me that footfall:
  Is my gloom, after all,
Shade of His hand, outstretched caressingly?
  "Ah, fondest, blindest, weakest,
  I am He Whom thou seekest!
Thou dravest[36] love from thee, who dravest Me."

The chase is over. The captive hears the voice of his Captor ringing about him: "Everything failed you because you ran away from me. Who would love a sinful mass of clay except me? I took everything from you not to make you unhappy but because I wanted you to seek them in my arms. You should not have excluded me from your love. I have preserved for you all the happiness I took away, and, now that you have surrendered, I will give it all back again."

The divine Victor in the race stands over him, and the captive now sees that the awful gloom which he thought must follow a surrender to the service of his Maker was only the shade of God's hand outstretched to caress and embrace him. Foolish he was and blind. He was driving out of his heart the very love and happiness he sought when he ran away from the loving Hound of Heaven.

34 *Bruit*: Clamor, din.
35 *Shard*: Broken pieces of pottery.
36 *Dravest*: Old form of drovest.